BEAUTIFUL
FALSE
THINGS

ALSO BY IRVING FELDMAN

WORKS AND DAYS

THE PRIPET MARSHES

MAGIC PAPERS

LOST ORIGINALS

LEAPING CLEAR

NEW AND SELECTED POEMS

TEACH ME, DEAR SISTER

ALL OF US HERE

THE LIFE AND LETTERS

BEAUTIFUL
FALSE
THINGS

POEMS

by

IRVING FELDMAN

GROVE PRESS

New York

Copyright © 2000 by Irving Feldman

Published simultaneously in Canada
Printed in the United States of America

FIRST EDITION

Library of Congress Cataloging-in-Publication Data
Feldman, Irving, 1928–
    Beautiful false things : poems / by Irving Feldman. — 1st ed.
      p. cm.
    ISBN 0-8021-3657-5
    I. Title.
   PS3511.E23B43   2000
   811'.54—dc21   99-38359
                                             CIP

DESIGN BY JULIE DUQUET

Grove Press
841 Broadway
New York, NY 10003

00   01   02   10 9 8 7 6 5 4 3 2 1

To
Natasha Anna
and
Alexander Martin
with my love

CONTENTS

ACKNOWLEDGMENTS

I wish to thank the John D. and Catherine T. MacArthur Foundation
and the National Endowment for the Arts for their support.

Some of these poems have appeared in the following magazines and
anthologies:

The Acre: "Praising Opens"

Confrontation: "Testing the Waters," "Desiring Power Where Surrender
Failed," "The Switch," "Sono un poeta . . . . Scrivo"

Gulf Coast: "Tantrum," "The Parting"

Kenyon Review: "Movietime"

The Nation: "Solange Mistral"

The New Yorker: "The Recognitions," "Voluptas," "*Les grandes passions
manquées*"

Oxford Quarterly Review: "Bust-up"

Paris Review: "These Memoirs," "Laura Among the Shades," "Lives of
the Poets"

Poetry: "Bad Brunch" (in different form), "Episode," "They Say and They
Repeat," "You Know What I'm Saying?" "The Retirement"

Raritan: "Of This and That, and the Other, and the Fall of Man," "Words
Out of Place"

Slate: "Joker"

Southwest Review: "Cartoons," "The Lowdown"

Western Humanities Review: "Oedipus Host"

Yale Review: "Beautiful False Things," "Wisdom (Not for Beginners),"
"City of Good Neighbors Blues"

"Movietime" appeared in *The Best American Poetry, 1998*

"You Know What I'm Saying?" appeared in *The Best American Poetry,
1997*

BEAUTIFUL
FALSE
THINGS

THE RECOGNITIONS

Not the god, though it might have been,
savoring some notion of me
and exciting the cloud where he was hidden
with impetuous thunderstrokes of summoning
—it was merely you who recognized me,
speaking my name in such a tone
I knew you had been thinking it
a long, long time, and now revealed yourself
in this way. Because of this, suddenly
who I was was precious to me.

VOLUPTAS

Strange to be remembering how
—was it twenty-odd years ago?—
you drew back from one of our kisses,
your head turning half away so that
I saw in our bedroom's half-light
your lovely profile and eye staring
out toward and into a passing thought.
Then all of half your smile was for me,
and you put your mouth to mine again
with overwhelmed gentleness.
We both were overwhelmed and pulled under.

Strange suddenly to remember this
after so many, many kisses,
after such years of rupturing.
Caught in our archaic caresses
(you know, that same old, old thing):
a space of five seconds of fresh time,
when nothing was happening
and nothing was happening yet.
And I now its voluptuary.

"SONO UN POETA . . . . SCRIVO"

At eighteen, nineteen, twenty years old,
my *Bohème* was a walk-up on Willett Street.
And I bolted up—two, three steps at a time
to my garret under the stars . . . where Mimì
came at me in the dark hallway, eyes burning.
I thought she'd strike me with her cold little hand.
Or darted back with angry mutters, and stood
in her apartment door, pronouncing my death
in hoarse, undecipherable arias.
She had lost the key—to everything.
Dark, small, white-haired, darting, a Fury
derided by minuter, madder furies.
Or was Catastrophe, the idiot Fate,
gibbering a million strands together.
Then swipe of the shears cuts a city short.
And all night just beyond my bedroom wall
something, newspapers, rustled into my sleep.
What is she doing? my sleep asked me.
Go to sleep, she's burning the building down,
looking by firelight for the key in the fire,
lost homeless wind groping among our embers.

                    *

Garret? Star-infested? On the Lower East Side?
Near the middle of the twentieth century?

Charming had it been, oh, say, something like
a set for the real thing—the opera, I mean
—with underwear filling in for window glass,
and nesting icicles in the potbellied stove,
and tarpaper shreds festooned overhead,
letting starlight fall through with the snow.
And yet, whatever scenery was shifted on
or off, the thrill was in the being there
and singing out, "Who am I? I am a poet!"
The air we sang was city soil, tenement musk:
cooking grease, coal dust, mildew, piss, sweat, rot.
Ages of human habitation, failure, loss
—birth-cries crowding on death-coughs in the walls—
authenticated our art and love and talk.
Come January, hallway johns froze over.
And under my kitchen sink, lath bared its bones
—one tough rat had knocked a chunk of plaster out,
and perched in the hole for a good long look around;
then, slumming god before my trite offerings,
turned up its nose, and faded into the wall,
as if to say, Keep it, kid—you need it all.
(Worse critics than the rat have condescended since.)
Picturesque? Of course—life imitates bad art.
Poor? Of course *not*—I was, we all were, *young*.

                    *

Kid poets, painters, actors, our collected works
you could have flushed down the hole of a pin,

but youth poured out of the holes in our clothes,
youth poured down from the openings in the heavens
—and poured on everything its shining *possible*.
We knew we were the whole show and theater:
authors, players, and the audience that counted.
And if we preened and played to one another,
we were the world's own preening to the universe,
admired in the bright, galactic galleries
—Because, we sang, we have the key, the key is
ourselves belovèd by and beyond everything.
And all the while, Mimì, like the *faux-phénix*
—cloud of ash and dust dying as it rises,—
Mimì, raving, scattered down on our heads
the starless, futureless snows of tomorrow.

                   *

Josie hemorrhaging her bank account
—she wants to give it away, set it free,
transfuse the whole world's neediness.
"Yesterday I went back there.
I brought these presents for my friends.
I have to rescue them—they have beautiful souls.
Bad things go on there. They hit people.
They wouldn't let an ex-patient in.
He was smiling at me as if I'm crazy.
I'm writing an exposé."
Mania only makes her insanely
tenderhearted, madly idealistic.
Are girls still that way these days, burning

in the furnace of the marketplace?
Thirty years after the year of our love,
ringing me out of nowhere,
from a thousand miles away, from Miami,
at two A.M., at three, at three-fifteen.
"They're out getting pizza.
I'm upstairs.
My sons have me locked in here
—the boys say they'll commit me again.
My baby's charged with child-molesting.
Because he put his hand on that little girl's tushie.
He isn't epileptic anymore.
He's such a beautiful young man.
My older one's a doctor.
I'm sneaking this call to you—I'm sorry.
I'm sorry. They're coming!
The soul is beautiful. You know that.
If anyone does, *you* do. You showed me that.
Can you help me, Irving?
Goodbye, Irving, goodbye."
The year of our love in New York—the year
you were so confused, so tormented, poor,
the year I could have been an ant fiddling,
so strange to you the semaphorings
of my inflamed adoration that left you
out in the cold, in the dark, asking
yourself—I still see it in your heavenly eyes—
"What does this boy want from me?"

. . .

I want to fall to my knees in the street
under your window where you stand half
in shadow, or half of you is shadow,
looking out, your lips moving.
I want to consummate my stupid conceit,
be blind in the white light of midday Miami.
I have no right, no right to see your ruin.
I understand nothing anymore.
It's all a mystery. I never understood.
Is this what crazy old Mimì
was raging over back there?
What she remembered? What she foresaw?
I have to save a blessing from the curse.
Somewhere, it has to be here somewhere.
Throw the key, Josie. Throw it down.
The soul is beautiful, the soul is beautiful,
you cried out from the heart of brutality.

Beautiful False Things

Broadcast as if from beyond the grave, a voice
is stumbling through a new vernacular
—some barbarous mouthplace of stumps and swamps
and ruts and roots and gulfs of rubble.
And, lurching toward you, urgent, unearthly,
this voice—imagine it!—is Dante's voice:
Dante declaiming Pinsky's *Inferno!*
Melodious and placeless bliss,
Paradiso, hasn't prepared him for this
his other afterlife—of fame,
this straining to illumine from within
a text he is always outside of.
And where he struggles isn't dark woods
but a bright, hellish glade of clear-cutting
and splintered slash where once the sweet words sang.

So Krip, the much-belaureled Yusuf Krip,
imagined one night in the groin of night
—when Mother Sleep, embittering her nipple,
banished him to wastes of consciousness.
Starving, parched for consolation—to float
at ease, a soul in a sea of sound,
and sip the medium of his being—
now, the friendly lamp beside him unlit,

deep in his study, seated, fingers gloved
in night, old Krip bestirred the radio.
Fiddled at a dial; poked a knob.
It glowed up ruby-red, blared into flame.
A spirit spoke: somewhere close, Dante—so near
he might have plucked at Krip's pajama sleeve—
was speaking English, no, talking American!

An agèd voice, frayed, failing.
Couldn't praising Heaven save the poet's throat?
Or lift his speech from its local self
to pure and universal eloquence?
But, torturer, devil, dunce, Dante's accent
loaded words with chains, shoved cadences down
to where the frenzied Unintelligibles
—like tongues torn out by the root midsentence—
go on expostulating in their Circle,
furious to transcend the interruption
and once and for all time get it said,
clamoring (if only one could know it!)
for the mercy of making sense.
                              And Krip
felt lost and bound in circles of his own,
straining to comprehend the delirious scene
—Dante clutching at this newfound Virgil who
was dragging him by the throat toward exile in
a world undreamt beneath his circling stars. . . .

                    *

He came to, chilled, laughing at himself.
A testimonial to the translation
from the author of the original?
What could he have been imagining?
Oh well, at 3 A.M. anything goes.
But Dante risen—on the radio?
Too much! Revived, more likely,
for purposes of pasta promotion.
Something was being sold. And whether pasta
or poetry, *Dante* guaranteed it!
—Oh, not the *Commedia*'s prophecy,
but "Dante having the Dante-experience!"

Amused, Krip pursued the fantasy:
the great poet, he who once was Dante,
trotted out from deep retirement in death
to perform the poet he no longer is,
authenticate words he never wrote
—on the road somewhere this very minute
starring in "My Life in Irony"
or, ironically, "The Death of the Author."
Better, then, to peddle secondhand poems
in postmodern America than reign
supreme in irrelevance on Parnassus?

Krip knew it, too, knew in his bones
how far the way from the grave,
and hard the translation to new life

—all this vehement clawing into
the glib slope of meaningless words.
But past a certain point Krip couldn't go,
embarrassed for Dante by the raw desire
of his voice, its urgency, its striving,
like the salesman selling himself to himself,
to rise from self-impersonation in
a single-throated rapture of conviction—not
to make sense (to whom here could Dante *wish*
to make sense?) but only to be believed.

The fantasy that shimmered before Krip
turned and stood in his path, roaring.
Painful to face Dante destitute,
Dante stripping himself to ease the way:
lifeworks reduced to vehicles,
and his history, his gravity,
the concern that made him who he was
—all this realm now streamlined to
a repertory of portable emotion,
a shorthand, a rhetoric, a kitsch,
soliciting the common adrenaline;
that, and the will, faithless, inconsolable,
to survive.
                    And then, sitting there, to sense,
behind the fever and banality,
Dante's mind was elsewhere, distracted, thinking,
Surely I wrote something once—but why?

Have I, too, abandoned everything to hope,
Krip asked, in order not to abandon hope?

"Hard the journey up and down other men's stairs?
Bitter to chew on, bitterer to swallow
other men's bread? But in this your new exile
you will be learning bitterest of all is
to savor your words with another's tongue.
Then welcome to our world, old wanderer,
where I, its resident exile, shall guide you,"
Krip rumbled back at the radio's rumble.
Not that Krip could savor much, not with
—rudely prosthetic on the stump of his own—
this stranger organ writhing in his mouth.
And he helpless, though he tried, to spit it out!
Sitting there, Krip spat dry-mouthed into the dark.

Gently, he depressed a button, and put out
the radio. He wanted it to go away.
Embarrassed for Dante? Now he could lay down
that burden, and go creep under it from shame.
Guide Dante? That was a laugh. And no kind one.
Krip growled suddenly, not to laugh that laugh,
or maybe to scare off the thing he'd understood
when he heard his voice and Dante's fall in step,
then coincide, like two shadows that blend
and darken together into a single shade
—who was himself, alone. That voice was *his*.

That accent's blundering teratogen
was his Albanian, not Dante's Florentine.
And that performance of author ecstasy,
that "heartfelt inauthenticity" were his.

No, not Pinsky's Dante, it was Pinsky's Krip.
A poem he'd written years and years ago.
Or was it someone else from that translator crew,
perhaps that Feldman kid—his latest Englisher?
To his Albanian ear, they were all
one indistinguishable "Feldminsky,"
and their "Feldminskish" some hypothesized speech,
the non-tongue of a nowhere—where, precisely,
personality is whited out, and into
the so-called and much beloved "works of Yusuf Krip."
Je est un autre? Oh, but in translations
je is beyond the incommensurate
—not sublime, just *personne*.

One leg, the left,
lay sunken and annulled in other otherness.
He willed it back. A shower of savage darts
got him out of his chair. Got him going
—three unsteady paces, then a lunging fourth
to the window, where he let the shade fly up.
One more infinite step beyond all this,
the "babies bright" of his infancy, the stars,
were afloat in their far-flung encampment.

All of it was sea. All of it was shore.
Where wanderlost is also homecoming.
Too early for dawn. Too late for sleep
—but lush and still, this hour of beginnings,
when (it was Krip's recurrent revery)

his sailors would be bearing Odysseus
out toward the circle of siren voices.
That crew a stepmother-tongue's wild brood
he'd scraped together from seaboard hellholes
in Egypt, in Lycia, and westward to Gaul
—day and night their dinning, brutish pidgin
drowned the water song, and tore the throat
from the wind and left the sky stifled,
world stunned with what they couldn't express.
Then midnight, once, plugging their ears,
Odysseus stopped their tongues.

Displaced and moving, and bound in place
unable to move, a pure desiring,
Odysseus, as blind, as large, as night,
listened—and music came, imbuing the dark
with his native speech, his mother tongue.
Everything he heard he understood
—chatter and tattle of water at its chores,
laving rock and laundering the stones,
in the warp of reeds, wind raveling
its gossip of laughter, shushing, whispers,

and spats and hisses and kisses and tears,
and wavelets' intimate tidbits of tidings,
water yielding to water enfolding water,
exchanging playful, sweet dependencies
—You need me I need you You'll feed me I feed you—
and song welling out from gratitude
the song was understood before it was song.
Odysseus here in oneness with
the world's eliciting intelligence,
the listening silence that moves our speech
—in the lush, still hour when, ravished, he drank,
and the speech that is the world came to his lips.

                    *

Too late for sleep. But sleepiness was, Krip knew,
the greater imperative. He would go to sleep.
And sleep—and tomorrow would write about
this last of his adventures, spewed up
out here beyond the Pillars of Hercules
by Time, the monster at the edge of the world.
He could smell the Albanian speech he loved:
of charcoal burners' huts below the pine-tree'd passes,
with smugglers and pack ponies adrift in haze,
and the agile stream telling the stones, darting
out of high solitudes to the salt-sharp beach.
The old excitement came, and fresh courage.
Could *taste* the tongue of Chako and Fishta—and Krip!
What to call the poem? "My Life in Irony?"

No. "My Life in Translation." No. Something else.
So, yes, he'll do this, though this poem, too,
in time will be recorded—by himself—
and flung broadcast through the great American night.
And Feldminsky would have all the last words.

     *

And drifting, in the embrace, on the bosom,
of Mother Sleep, Krip, drowsy, murmuring
in the world's ear, You'll never know, but, people,
believe me, it's better . . . the original.

Solange Mistral

Ange, tu m'as connu!

I knew that silhouette elegant in black,
that arm upraised, hailing, and stepping toward
a cab in the furious street . . . who, reaching
to pull the door shut, turned in my direction
—but not, after forty years, the haggard rock,
the supernatural contour of her face, and eyes
as if they'd looked on the purely evil and
utterly boring so long that evil bored
and boredom was itself their only evil.
Then the charred gaze fell blankly on me
—from the blackened stones of a wayside shrine,
an empty place where someone once died
and a last gasp of smoke now clutches at
the luckless, halted passerby, demanding,
Did you think you amused me, fool?
Yes, I, too, had scraped my match, burned and moved on.
After trial by fire is trial by ash.
I bow to the verdict of the embers.

TESTING THE WATERS

Daylong and then in dreams this testing
the waters—how swift, sweet, thick the course
of things, how cool, consistent, various,
and what the current bears, or bypasses—
so that we can go on and on in the swim
and still be staunch and other than this flowing:
not carried away, not left behind.

These Memoirs

Stumbling midnight tipsy in Jackson's studio,
who knocked black paint over into tomorrow
and throbbing rainbows of our morning after?
Well, thanks to these *Memoirs*, now we know.

When howling sounded over Rockland State,
whose Parker jotted the holy phonemes down?
'Fess up, Allen, and give the man back his pen!
—because these *Memoirs* tell us, and now we know.

In that smoky predawn dive *who* taught Balanchine
to do the twist, quoted since on scores of stages?
No thanks to Mr. B. we know about this
—down to the bubbles in the Veuve Cliquot.

There could have been dull Nothing, you never know
—bland canvas, numb poem, torsos untorsed.
Who, then, was the quirk at the lip of Oblivion,
the droplet that set the trembling source aflow?

But by what inversion of Fate the Ironist
have his loveliest strokes become his erasure?
Surest to remember is soonest forgot.
That's the awful truth, as these *Memoirs* show

—fitfully, from darkening pages, where one reads
how, years ago, overlooked, *his* drained goblet lay
tipped over, losing light, filling with silence,
far below the lid of Cage's black piano.

"And lies there still, flowing, lost, overflowing,"
our nameless author wrote. His last words are:
"Absurd though all this will seem, yet in these pages
Oblivion toasts Memory now—as we know

"this moment, overflowing, flowing, lost."

Laura Among the Shades

Honor, and excellence, and transcendent best,
I was the laurels I denominated:
diadem and queen and diadem's bearer.
Disdaining tribute from inferior hands,
I crowned myself *The Greatest Poet Alive.*

And died to pursue opponents far worthier.
I bore my distinction against the famous dead,
and grimly—not their rival, their enemy.
My evergreen shall overgrow their names
grimed on the black page of Oblivion.

My conceit was always larger than myself.
Not vainglory, it was ambition, and meant
to show my complete contempt for poetry.
Accursed the leaves I plucked and poison to me,
my laurels mingled with berries of the nightshade.

LIVES OF THE POETS

Poor Paul—when he might have been kind
to a kid, he made a pass instead.

Well, literally zillions of passes
are launched all the time: by day and by night
hot dragon pantings, pawings, pinches, winks,
insinuating, sucking smooches like silks
ripping deliciously from throat to crotch,
lewd, obvious leers and gross eyeballings,
and quiet invitations to dinner, drinks
—all throng the atmosphere around the planet
till Eros gasps for air, blanches, blushes.
This very second dozens hundreds thousands
of passes are dying to get themselves laid
to rest in the worst ways imaginable.
And while most fall flat and pass away,
some, believe it or not, make out, connect.
And who's to say the world should be different?
Then was Paul's especially brutal? Hardly.
Undeniably importunate? Puh-lease!
Or something like a minor herbivore
trespassing on its munching way? Perhaps,
perhaps—if one could ask the grasses.
Really, as passes go, it was prosaic

—a small *éclat* of soul's wind, like the ghost
of affection absent, chill, and odorless
but for its fetor of self-absorption.
(If Eros heard it, did he hold his nose,
and utter some rudeness in return?
Or let it pass, as manners ask one to?)
Puff, it was present; *piff*, it was past.
But piffling though it was, and pitiful
—imagine, if you will, a pass on day leave
from an orphanage or hospital—and brief
and too impeccably impersonal
to be malicious, still it wasn't kind.

                    *

Sunny afternoon (May? June?) in 'forty-six.
Fifth-floor cold-water walk-up on Orchard Street.
I'm a student slash poet slash bohemian.
The world is all before me. I laugh a lot.
My spirits too high for whatever turns up,
and "greatness" the afflatus fluttering my tongue,
I'm at that age: unable to distinguish
ardent idealism from ambition
from rebelliousness from my sense of fun.
I add my dash of satiric slash fervid fizz
to the Lower East Side's postwar bubbling scene
—where my signature is swirled off into
the *Zeitspritz* of the many-minded foam.
. . .

Paul, at twice my seventeen, is slash nothing.
He's fully hyphenated, poet-novelist-
playwright-critic-teacher, but unstuffy, boyish,
and like a boy responsible to truth only
and to his pleasure. He's one of us, our best:
self-styled Socrates and wonderful *Überkind*
(whom success alone will save from ending as
resentful *Untermensch*): our David, our champion,
doing in the dinosaurs of Authority
—with uncredentialed, free-lance brainpower,
the look-ma-no-hands of the genial amateur.
His surefire dialectical judo pretzels
the bully in bully's own dumbbell stranglehold.
Once he shows those dads they're extinct, they'll just *go*.
He's got the word on everything—including,
quite possibly, me? I admire so much
I copycat this man I scarcely know.
And now he's dropped by, dying, as he says,
to hear me read aloud from my *oeuvre*.
Will I do that for him?

                                    Why, certainly, sir.
Pages gripped in one hand, about to begin
—when suddenly he lunges for the other
like someone really dying, clawing for help,
drowning, going under, heart infarcted,
hand hemorrhaging mortality at every pore.
And I'm to lift him out? To stanch the bleeding?
But *no*, my hand's apparently a telephone
connecting heart to heart, and he's calling up.

Look! as if to filter visual static
from aural ecstasies to come, his lids have shut.
Charade of a soul in transport, wholly tuned in
—to whom I sit reciting every blessèd one
of my twenty, precious, tender, teeny poems.
And all the while something odd is going on.
What he appropriates, promptly I disown.
My person redefines itself at the wrist.
If he wants whatever it is, here, take it!
My arm's offended by this stupid mitt.
Pluck it off! Anyway, I could care less
—I'll grow another, new, strong, articulate.
And the rest of me will get away clean!
(But if, nerve-damaged, numb, the stump should stay
humorless, unmusical . . .)

My reading done, I get to see Paul do
his Act II: reluctant opening of eyes
—tearing himself from the pure Ineffable.
Affably, perhaps myopically, too, a bit,
he talks down his nose toward where I'm waiting:
sly nods, knowing winks at my Unconscious,
things to make me doubt I am who I think,
have me think I'm a stranger to myself.
However distant his acquaintance with either,
he's willing to present us to each other.
That seems to be the offer. Think it over.

. . .

What I think is my hero doesn't play fair.
And doesn't understand me, not for a second.
I don't aspire to be an object of
his interest, or even noticed especially.
What I want is to hang around and admire,
and learn all his sharp intellectual moves,
those quick grips and nifty throws I can use
to flip the world over onto its back,
and hold it down until it cries out, Uncle!
What I think? Master protects disciple.
The slugger doesn't hit on the batboy.
And here he's put *me* in danger—from himself—
prevaricating interest in my poetry.
Oh, I'll go on admiring the guy, but never will
forgive him his treachery.

                        Is what I thought.

            *

That, roughly, was fifty years ago,
and half these years Paul's been gone—and half
his mourners have by now outrun mourners
of their own, and taken cover in the ground.
And so here one is between two corteges,
Paul's past and the present writer's assembling
(slowly, gentlemen!) somewhere up ahead.
Well, Paul had his decade or so in the sun,
his nearly fifteen years of fame

—which at this distance seem foreshortened
to Andy's famous "fifteen min."
The times took his hand and walked with him
a while, a mile. And then walked on.
His coronary when it came along
was wholehearted, unrefusable.

Wisdom (Not for Beginners)

When I was ten and seven
I heard a wise man say,
"'We err just to live on a little.'"

That would have been Paul, our Socrates, who
at thirty-five was swiftly approaching wisdom,
and soon would reveal to us—with shy aplomb,
as if requiring himself to tell a truth
too obvious to mention—that his Sagehood was
a rumor no more, but full-fledged, in full flight,
and about to land not simply with good advice,
but also making itself available
to the world as an example day and night.
And, really, when you got right down to it,
could anyone rather be wrong than be Paul?
(*Some* errors, then, were perhaps *extravagant?*)
It wasn't just the Goethe he kept quoting;
his *tone*, wistfully sighing, artlessly prim,
befitted wisdom suffered for, wisdom won.
And I, tenderfoot among the symposiasts,
I sighed louder than all the rest, and hushed
—to hear the feathered, strange *whoosh*, the susurrus:
Wisdom's wing was buzzing our coffee-klatsch.
Yes, yes, awestruck, we agreed, life is tough!
It never occurred to me to laugh and sing

seeing a stuffed owl cosily lecturing
—that self-pity warmed over by self-approval.
Because "we?" That would have been Goethe and he.
However thoughtlessly you and I screw up
our lives, and trash the people around us,
Paul, poor guy, had to force himself to err
—with difficulty outwitting his wisdom,
though wisely, of course, for the best of reasons.
And "err," that had to be the harmless stuff
that leaves you ready to go and goof some more,
the way a hobby might, or small addiction.
Persistent fools and great sinners needn't apply
—assuming they think they require licensing.
Then "live on a little" would mean: *less and less?*
A dreary kind of wisdom—though who knows
what might inspire the aspirant narcissist
to grand, to noble, to daring self-regard?

And me? I've lived on a little.
And now I am five-and-sixty
—with no idea where I've gotten to,
but know some things I should apologize for.

Honors! Prizes! Awards! Etc!

Eternal outsider always wanting in
rattles the latch, enters the cell, rummages
for, reaches after, some unimaginable
innermost . . . lets the body drop . . . reaches into
your body, into mine . . . trying to know
what it cannot understand: ungraspable life!
Or we build a body here of many bodies,
a club, a corporation, a membership
of Immortals in a Muses' Institute,
closing ranks against, precisely, *that one,*
who (though widely acknowledged *mighty* and *dreadful,*
and present as the night—self-nominated—
between the lines of every short list
for all the prizes and honors under the sun)
is turned away repeatedly at the door
as inadmissible, as having this bad rep
for hopping into the sack with anyone
—muddy old parvenu dragging people down to
his level, into his unspeakable hovel. . . .
And we make a party—a gala's galaxy
rubs the elbows it bends to toast itself,
and crowds together to a massive shining:
no chink, no aperture, no slightest silence
where to enter, where to hunker in and hide

—only our animated, general hubbub,
and overhead more-than-mortal outcries from
the laurel branches of our green academy.
Who hasn't hoped to be more famous than death?

OEDIPUS HOST

Blindman, cripple quarrel in a single body
over which one leads, which will stumble after.
Each step's disaster—somebody's trampled under,
half trips the other forward, half drags him back.
Back on top now, he kicks out, tumbles over.
Blind pride precedes the fall, lame pride plucks up
the fallen feller, and pushes him on ahead.
How long has this? How long has *he?* How much *longer?*
you ask—and love the man for all this way he's come.
And pity those bare and bruised and swollen feet.
How *far?* Twelve steps? Twelve *monster* steps, for sure
—farther than from Glorious Greece of yore to us.

The *Hindenberg* bursting into radio flames.
Welles's *War of Worlds.* Murrow covering the Blitz.
Welch lambasting McCarthy. Kennedy's cortege.
Now add the day that *he* first guested on a "talk."
Moments truly Great in Broadcast History.
And I was there. Tuned in. Glued to my set. Taping.
That video's in my personal collection.
And now he hosts his own I never miss a show.
Curtain rises: for one agonizing minute
a spot wanders lost, then falls on him, and brightens.
You could have heard the light creeping on the floor,
it was so quiet there. Now everything busts loose.

Even the cams get hot, can't pan fast enough, *bam
bam,* zap from face to awe-gone face, then shoot
the audience going off its collective nut.
He's in his trademark toga—sun-blighted, rain-splotched.
He totters, shuffles, wobbles, he staggers, lurches
—his old drapery coughs up centuries of dust,
like a winding sheet wind-uplifted from the earth.
As if drum-majoring a weird parade of one,
he waves, thumps his pilgrim staff. *Cudgel's* more like it,
good for beating back the mean-assed roadside curs.
You can just bet that stick has busted up a few.

Whoever did his makeover's some kind of brain.
That mask he wore is gone; this face is mask enough.
How could paint improve the hollows of those cheeks,
the dark sumps pooled inside the sockets' crusty holes,
those hoary locks the gore has plastered into place?
They say his wardrobe stocks a dozen changes
—it takes that long to launder out, and *in,* the dust.
Onscreen some ancient rock, a gnarled old tree,
sun-baked villages, moonscape vistas frozen white,
where, montaged, his ghostly slo mo figure stalks, stalks
—stuff so *un*contemporary you can't believe
one stringy hand is clutching on a microphone.
He's like oblivious, like he couldn't care less,
his stagger's that unwavering, his trance so deep.
One gentle daughter brings the guests onstage.
The other's in another show . . . she turns the wheel. . . .

*

I think those girls must love their dad a lot
to lead him all this way. I had daughters once. . . .
Two were rotten bad; the good one went and died.
And once I owned a country, a little one
—the car, the house, garage, the job, the family.
Hell with that! Now look at me, bedridden
in Brooklyn, shut in, on disability.
Fate fucked me over. It got me good.
Feet don't work. Eyes going out of business.
Someday soon I'll be down to audio.
Twice a week Mrs. Pomerantz looks in
—my cranky lifeline; could be better herself.
Not that I let on she has me worried.

So when *The Oedipus Hour* rolls around
it's all right, it's okay. Job and Lear drop by,
dressed in the clothes they actually wore.
Or it's Don Q.—the piercing eyes, the broken lance.
Think you've seen a lot? They've seen it *all*.
Or Julius Caesar calmly matching up for us
the holes in his toga to his awful stabs.
So let 'em, those critics, jump all over the show
—for "bad taste," for "frankly, implausible."
Lots of losers from history come on
—also everyday survivors, sinners, ex-cons,
and handicapped, and freaks, and fatties so shy
they go transparent not to weigh on people's eyes.

And some real trash who piss on your sympathy.
He welcomes them—in, like, his living room.
Each guest's escorted to a chair. They sit down.
Hang out. Talk back and forth. Tell their stories.
Pain this one saw, that one suffered, other gave.
You see them let go, feel at home, forget their acts.
Forget to be impatient. Really listen.
Don't make faces, interrupt, drown the other out,
talk behind their hands. Show nothing but respect.
Like they're telling us, World is plenty harsh
—critical will only make it harsher.
Restless Oedipus goes silent among them,
a tall needle stitch-stitch-stitching it together.

And sometimes people's stories meet—then wonder
widens their eyes, the worry leaves their brows.
You were there? . . . So that was *you*! . . . Of *course*,
   I was. . . .
That happened to *me!* . . . And me. . . . Can you
   believe it? . . .
Now it happens to *you*. You're here, and you're there, too.
Because anyone's story could be everyone's story.
Something tremendous is going on tonight.
Everybody's coming out to everybody.
Even coming out to us, to *me*, out here.
Can anyone not feel what I feel in my heart
so strong the wave of it rolls back to *them*?

Because no longer are we putting people down
for creep, dog, dickhead, weirdo, whatever.
That's over. Done with. Ashamed I did.
The shut-ins, everything shut in, are coming out.
The fatties step in front of their flesh and shout,
Look your fill—I'm so big no closet can hold me!
Lying here, I stomp and hoot and high-five them on.
And feel America's big heart in my heart pumping.

A new thought thrills right through me—my precious power
I squeezed out and saved up from any scrap of luck
I ever got my hands on, got control of:
my secret privileges; leeways I give myself;
meannesses just for the hell of it;
rewards I'll take and nibble from my fingertips
—yes, my edge in life that puts me one up
over anyone who thinks that I'm this nothing
and can't do my chunk of damage, if I have to:
yes, goodbye my self-intensive-care unit,
I'm getting off you, my bitter, my sweet life support!
I, *we*, are saying,

               Dear down-and-outers,
never again will you have to envy us.
Not you. Not you. Not you. Not you. Not you.
Do you understand? You . . . no . . . envy . . . me!
I spell it out like talking to a child.
Speaking the same words, but it's a new language!

*

It's Sunday night. It's ten to ten. On the dot.
Spokespersons about to get into their pitches.
Noises scuffle behind. Bumps and bulges—like
the curtain's alive inside. Head pokes it open.
Then Oedipus pushes through. His travel cloak
looks mussed and crooked. He's erect, tilted forward,
fighting the wind and the dark way uphill.
Pounds his staff three times. Pounds it three times more.
Those bitter slits get right up in the camera's face,
look it dead in the eye. Just when we feel our hearts
surrendering, thunder—caught, struggling—flashes free!
All over America on millions of sets
Oedipus again now makes the same speech.

"God-marked, who looks at me

                        sees the god-power.
Apollo adopted,

            marked me in the cradle,
breaking my feet;

            marked me with my hands,
taking my eyes;

            taking my eyes, my hands snuffed
the sun, the farseeing;

              not to see myself seen,
I covered my shame in shadow;

                shadow is

my greater shame

                 —darkness I made lord of light.

On broken feet, in darkness,

                        feeling for the way

I came here seeking,

                     now shall creep away seeking

never this suffering again,

                     but bright death

where (where?) your light-arrows

                         open my eyes,

Apollo."

        *

Gone now. They came for him, his mom and dad.
Out of nowhere. Out of the flies, it looked.
The pair of them were standing in this bucket.
People still talk UFO. Me, I think it was
a cherry-picker thing. I'm guessing, rented.
Down smooth as butter they ride to him onstage.
Whatever anyone wrote, no way they're dead.
Bloody-red, the bucket door swings open.
Blind, he hasn't a clue what's going on.
Broke my heart to see him standing stump-still,
except his old head, yawing like a horse's.
Like smelling at the sights he couldn't see.
Then out they step. Dad's beard is white, and trim
—around the purple zigzag of a cicatrice.
The mom is old enough to be his mom.

Gasp, the studio goes. I'm gasping, too.
Somehow, without our knowing it, we *knew,*
Something *major's* going down. And him?
All that pride is bent in one big question mark.
Like he's asking Fate, *Now what you got in store?*
The old battler, he pulls himself together.
He straightens up, his whole body expressing,
I took your best shot once—can take it once more.
Suddenly, this big smile. It's like teeth can see.
Then sweet-tongued Ismene's laughing, oh god,
can't hold back her laughter—so bubbling-happy
with something she knows that I'm laughing, too.
"Surprise, Papa! Guess who's here to see you!"
Black pit of his mouth opens. He's speaking.
"Apollo, golden Phoebus, great lord of sun
and death, is that you in your bright chariot?"

Desiring Power Where Surrender Failed

1. RIDDLE

How can sharing bread not be true companionship?
When a shit-eater has you dine from his dish.

2. CEREMONY

More awful than the banquet of excrements
was his toastmasterly regurgitation
praising your compelled "collegiality";
then the brown buss of his lips on your cheek;
then round your neck and hung at heart level to hide
the shame and vomit: the cold weight of his medal.

3. HONOR

His one principle is this: he will accept
no wage or fee until he's begged for it.
So you see him shove forward, cup in claw,
and genuflect to the dribbling cloaca
—always the proud first in line for seconds.

4. "HE KNOWS THE SYSTEM AND
HOW IT WORKS"

First, subsumption upward of the small fry
defying gravity in the next greater's gut;
then—presidential, chairmanly, veepish,
at every stage more pure, more unnourishing—
the voiding downward and processing of shit.
This is how it works, he knows, snacking below,
repossessing himself as this fungible stuff,
while his gloat says, "Who dines on me dines on dreck."

5. DESIRING POWER WHERE
SURRENDER FAILED

Shit Happens! the bumper sticker fleeing the scene
hurls back, thumbing its rear at the victim.
Where his mouth used to be, tire tread grimaces
the collusive smirk of his admit-it-Jack-
you-like-it-too, and a taste for collision.
Resurrected as the vehicle, brutal,
but weak, he's driven to revisit that instant:
its slow approach, then sudden wreckage,
when Power ran his innocence down
and had some buttered roadkill for lunch.
So he thinks to pass you through him
and serve you to yourself from his dish
—and observe you observing your principles
become secondary, lax, late, corrupt;

then self-surrender turns self-loathing,
and self-loathing a greed for more spoiled self;
then you fleeing your corpse in the road, grinning.

6. HAPPENS *NOT!*

No, you decline the company of Power: stooge,
suck-up, cynic, panegyrist, footstool, wrecker
—who, caught in some eternal happening of shit
in hell, struggle, and can't engorge, can't expel
the truth that punishes their enfeebled craws.
You give yourself, give more—do your uttermost.

7. ENVOI

Go, little poem, go far away from here!
—before he comes to covet your rebuke,
and butts you down and rolls around in you
and smears you over himself and gulps you in.
Run, little poem, run, run away from here!

The Switch

Each of us has it—the live/die switch:
oiled daily, recalibrated, kept ready,
hair-trigger, or unbudgeable—maybe—
until in one instant kindness, care, compassion,
love, self-sacrifice swing sickeningly
toward . . . *past* indifference, past hostility . . .
toward *nothingness*. It trips. And "*You*," we think,
"you've been here too long, too noisily.
You're in the way. You interfere. Dying?
Well, don't just hang around here screaming
and pulling those sad faces of yours—do it!
And, yes, we'll tidy up for you a bit."

Even this child at play, he knows it's there
somewhere near or *in* his own dear mother's heart.
And if he can be a little bad, a little,
a little badder, he will *help* her find it
—in the dark, among tears, at the threshold where
an empty, thrilling *puff* replaces him.

Tantrum

From the doorway he saw the next room
was empty, so empty that if he *were*
to step inside it would remain empty
—unless by means of this chaos he should
almost almost inhabit it, though never
in any form be able to leave.

Of This and That, and the Other, and the Fall of Man

This and that.
Here and there.
And me.
We're okay
where we are.
I've got this.
And I want that—badly.
This is red and round.
That is round and red.
I can get that
if I poke it with this.
No, I'll have to throw this
to dislodge that.
Good shot!
Here comes that.
There goes this.
Come here, you luscious round red thing!
Poor this, it's gone now.
Absent. Offed. *Pfft.*
Actually, I was rather fond of this.
If only this had been that
—or that this!
Now I hate this.
You deserved your fate, this.

So don't blame me.
It could have been you, you know.
It didn't *have* to be that.
You could have made me want you more.
But no, you wanted to deprive me
of your red roundness.
Bad this, shame on you!
wherever you are, out there,
thinking you're just fine,
a perfect little this.
And now that is all gone.
No more that.
I want this, I want that—badly.
But this this won't be that this.
That that wasn't this that.
I didn't know.
I know.
Oh, I'm being lifted up.
Yow!
I'm being thrown!

CARTOONS

Somewhere cars are parking any which way.
Somewhere else some cars are doing any damn thing,
getting all over the place and getting into stuff.
Some quarter- or half-acre of open space, some *lot*
—cars are going in and getting right on top of it.
And they're bringing bumpers and fenders *this* close.
Cars are coming and going *just as they please.*
Some cars are doing it day and night and *overnight!*
Doesn't anybody *care* what's going on there and *there* and *there?*
It's time someone put up some signs—*don't you think?*

      *

A whizz-by of words down a leafy street;
big red letters peering over the green slats
of the brand-new, bright, shiny pickup truck
—just loafing along and hanging out, at ease
in the still momentum inside the commotion,
just going with the flow of trees and trellises
and whatever else is streetwise in spring:
seven signs in search of seven sites,
where they shall proclaim NO PARKING to the world,
and—with two words and by the power to seize
chattels, assets, persons—make a sacred space.

But, for now, the prohibitions are as happy
as grown-ups who are being as happy as kids.
On holiday from making sense, and taken out
of every context, they kick back and hang loose,
take it all off, right down to their coats of paint.
Out of character now—as mere characters—
they're so mellow you could drive a twenty-six-wheeler
loaded up with universe between "N" and "O."

                    *

PARKING RESTRICTED OFFENDERS WILL BE TOWED
UNDER PENALTY OF LAW ALL OTHERS KEEP OUT
Block letters on the sign's brow mean, I mean business.
Mean, None of your cursive crawling charm crap for me.
No Pretty-please-I'll-be-your-best-friend-I-promise.
No Tickle-my-belly-while-I-lick-your-hand.
This is monomania's forbidding scowl
—its pliers for getting a good grip on its head.
And it *must* be awful being ripped away
from the great ingathering of everything
and raised up high to tell the All to toe the line.
Meanwhile, cars flaunt their flouting, screeching out fast,
skidding on curves, squealing, when not crashing, to stops,
and honking their heads off every chance they get
—all to shout, Hey, make yourself at home with us,
and let your scarlet letters brighten our lot!
And air is airier, space more spacious now.
One corner of the sign sports a lost left mitten.
At its foot a hubcap *clank-clink-clunks* itself down.

WORDS OUT OF PLACE

Somewhere, say, a slip-slopping mash or mush
or bubbling bog of abandoned name tags
on a ballroom floor frugging the wee hours through.
Pop. Sigh. Balloons release their airy souls.
Prepare themselves for damper, graver spirits.
A streamer untwists its silvery slight being.
The silent flotilla sways to the gurgles
of the gala's ankle-deep, salt, cold champagne,
sloshes knee-high now in the great gashed vessel
—doing a last dance with A with B with C. . . .
Nearby, nameless swimmers in darkness kick out,
thrashing in the seawind-tormented wash . . . when

the stenciled life raft of a NO SWIMMING sign,
sky-high atilt atop the last wave in the world,
comes drop-drop-dropping into range, in reach.
Some avid readers—keen-eyed, and literate,
and literal-minded, and obedient—
get it brilliantly and for dear life hang on.

                *

And somewhere for a while a wind forsakes
a leaflet blown against some desert rocks.
Wind, wind has gone away—gone back for more.
One leaflet face up under the sunny azure.

Surrender! Surrender! Surrender Your City!
Or Suffer! Suffer! Suffer Consequences!
the page cries out to the populace of sand.
Gingerly, three jackals hearken, and sniff.
Lift up heads and ask the sun.
Ask wind, Wind, whereof do you speak?
Delicate, astute, tongue touches *S*.
Snake bit? Worm stung? Home.Quick.Tongue.Come.
—Smoke! And,yes,squiggle,of . . . mm,mm . . . *sangre.*

Alpha (first), then Beta, then Gamma initial
selfsame with showers of fine flourishes,
attesting Alpha, et al.—the real guys
and brothers, true owners, heirs and sole assigns
in perpetuity of turf hereabouts
and out as far as eye sees from boulder yon
to yonder scree—have read and duly noted *Stuff.*

*

The fierce maenads of existence keep tearing
The Dictionary into deep, inscrutable
blizzards of Orphic confetti, swirling up,
and down on the stream parading its passage.
And, loveliest foam, the syllables, riding, sing
this moving beauty of the moment's novel body.
Nor will the river be as it was
before words were set to water.

THE LOWDOWN

Remember when Jack changed girls year by year?
And how we talked it up—and talked it down?
Our tongues deliberated every sigh and vow.
Let no fact go unlubricated to its grave,
no innuendo stay unmaterialized:
real dirt was the grist our guts required.
Gossip grain by grain was how we earthworms prayed
—communion with clay that churned up ground of being
into sweaty partoosies of particulars:
Who was carrying the torch? Who was tinder?
Who had the ball? the balls? the gism? the juice?
Who had it? the speck? the spark? the dough? the power?
we wanted to know—since we *knew* it was *somewhere*.
And where was it going? Who'd have it tomorrow?
Remember that? And don't you remember when
dear Jill's affairs were *everyone's* affair?

Then history moved on, went off to live
in other loins and pairings of pantings.
Hear that furor of rumors rumbling underground?
Not elegies, for sure, but music of
the *new* historians' delirious mucosa.
Our chatter's like this here crumbling incoherence.

Our cohort's down and done for. So who gives a damn
about these temporary contemporaries
—not you, not I—now that Jack's nurse changes Jack,
and Jill, still carrying on, changes doctors!

JOKER

"Call!" "Call!" "Call!" "Call!" "Call!" "Call!"
Thought I was bluffing. Wanted to see me.
I'm loaded, guys, I am fuller than full.
So, see 'em, read 'em, feed 'em, eat 'em—and weep!
Then, our heart-and-soul-satisfying smart sharp
snap-and-slap-the-cards-on-the-table shtick;
up on two feet, I cracked the buggy whip my wrist;
and the five-of-a-kind of the hand I held high,
one by one, Take that, *whump!* and Take that, *whamp!*
and Take this, *whomp!* I smacked down—notice served
to all the stiffs and to the Big Stiffer
by the woodcutter and master of the deck,
owner of the ax, last man alive and standing!
So I chastised Bad Luck's obstreperous butt
—the table back bearing up the scarred baize.
Ground of our gaming, I stung him good,
taught him who boss is and damn you hold still
while we game on, hand after hand forever,
our give and take sluicing the lucre pure.

And leaned across, raking the heap home to Papa,
my forearm's enormous promontory engulfing
the golden louis, the silver simoleons;
and looked around, to share this big win
in my eyes, and saw what everyone was seeing:

my aces aging, fading, suddenly blank,
like the Killer Joker sprawled faceless there,

and on the loose now, and running wild
from the shattered room in the house of ashes.

MOVIETIME

They can't wait. ("We couldn't wait," they'll say.)
And that's not the only thing the lovers can't do.
They seem unable to get their clothes off in time,
or to catch the breath they're losing in each other's mouth.
Oddly, they've lost the knack of getting into a bed
without keeling over onto the floor in a tangle
of bedclothes and other clothes. (Fabric can be so stupid!)
If only they could get out of each other's way
or at least into each other's ways in the right way.
And they can't slow down, and clearly can't go fast enough
to catch up to what they're feeling—maybe if something had
some texture, but things slide by, going far too fast.
Can't they sort of go back to point zero and start over?
Really, they seem like strangers who can't get acquainted
and who, by trying harder, get stranger and stranger.
God only knows what they *can* do; probably it's just
whatever this is they're doing now, crashing into each other
at this impromptu intersection they've just created.
If nothing happens soon, we're afraid they'll start *honking*.
Can't *someone* stop a sec to gasp, "Pardon me" or "After you?"
Well, let's hope it's all clearer to them than it is to us

("Can't we *please* have a *little* more light?" we find we're
    praying)
—even though we've been in that position ourselves,
in those positions, in a dark room some suddenly wild night
with scream after scream about to push past everything.

It seems, then, profoundly artful (while perfectly banal)
for the camera to leave them to their breathless inventories
and ferocious ineptitude they're getting better at
—by cutting to an all-night art-deco beanery
and its fat lone diner, a placid and famous detective,
who's sitting there and simply, competently eating.
Seeing food on the screen of this dark, musty movie house
isn't exactly the most appetizing thing in the world.
Still, his fork's unerring in finding the way to his mouth;
his spoon never winds up depositing chowder in his ear.
Feats of coordination we can say we, too, have mastered.
So we especially enjoy seeing his gestures glide
between sheer slobbery and icky, self-conscious prissiness.
A common achievement, commonly taken too lightly.
Of course, what's-his-name actually (if that's the word) doing
    this
is even more famous, so the interplay of disguise
and guise (that actor sampling what, and while, this gumshoe
    eats,
for example): this teases and fascinates on its own.
To suspend our disbelief would be to lose the "beauty part,"

this magical uncertainty of "takes" doubled and trebled.
Now the sensitive, round, good-natured face looks troubled.
From under his eyebrows, the camera peers deeply into
a too-clear water glass and jumbo portion of tapioca,
a soiled, creased paper napkin; it swings around, up,
and scans the blue tracery of neon in the mirrors.
So many, many clues—and not a single crime in sight!
When camera pulls away, that's him there in the middle of
the mess, calmly, reassuringly to us, ruminating.
What was total alien jumble is starting to reveal
to him certain underlying kinships: it's coming together.
His smile says it all: Digestion doing fine, thank you.
He taps a finger on the formica—oh, ever so lightly.
With chaos, it implies, you take your time, *you take your time*.
Okay, we'll wait around with him, we can be patient, too.
One A.M. Two A.M. And everything is going slower.
Out there, something set in motion is slowing down.
He's standing up—must be time to go. But go where? Do
    what?
He pays the bill, so slowly we can count out change clinking
over the cashier's ritual, "Button up, Buddy, it's cold
    tonight."
"Bud," maybe. No one's called him *Buddy* since Pappy died.
"How come?" his face asks with such eloquent perplexity
we're cracking up, we're rolling around. He's beautiful!
(And, hey, did you glom on to the size of that tip he left?)

Outside, morning paper under his arm, he's walking away,
doing that endearing, flatfooted toddle of his.
Oh my, didn't we know it, he's one of those *graceful* fatties!
On the deserted street, he stops a second, short of breath
(poor guy, we think, this *isn't* acting!), and is almost around
the corner and lost from view, when we realize

how happy we are with all these tiny textures of being
and time the fat guy has generously treated us to
—so many moments to talk over and appreciate,
bits of personality we'll rescue from time's rush-rush
(and from the damned plot always trying to do itself in).
Which is why we like to beat the crowd by leaving early
—before masks drop and the whole thing runs smack into its
    ending,
and, stunned, everything is itself, nothing more, nothing else.
Because, isn't this what movies are for?—offering large
and variegated surfaces of hard-to-figure-out depth
to our revery's minute, pleasurable inspection,
to savoring and recollection and repetition,
so that our minds move around more than the movie does,
quickly from moment to moment, but slowly within it.

Strolling home on the peaceful, lamplit, empty avenue,
we try out a wide waddle, a pigeon-toed toddle—and then
remember that right about *now* the lovers are rousing

and whispering across the world rifting between them
what, arm in arm, you and I, it so happens, are murmuring,

"Was it good for you?" "Mmmm. And you? Was it good for
    you?"

HEAVENLY MUSE

Et le regard qu'elle me jeta
me fit baisser les yeux de honte

Late, as usual.
And staging her entrance
—the flung-off mac flying into
a little storm of its own making;
wellies kicked to a corner,
as if reproached for the rain;
the flowered brolly dropped, upended,
weeping on the welcome mat.
"I'm drenched—*literally*
soaked right to the bone!"
Not that she couldn't do
without drama, but so intent
her sense of self,
theater happened around her.
Things snapped to attention,
aware all at once they, too, were there,
and eager to answer her vehemence.
And I no less, no less so.

Subdivided, firelit, a crowd
of raindrops was the fine glitter
in the dark auburn of her hair.
"You're a little late, you know,"

I called out toward where she'd gone off,
sweeping the vividness after her.

"Sarcasm is beneath me—it's rude.
Make certain it's beneath you, too.
I'm *very* late, thank you
—as I very well know."
My john door at its most rumblingly prim.
And here she was in the room again,
refurbished, radiant, and ticked.
"Please to repeat what you said."

"I *said*, 'You've kept me waiting
—miserably, if you must know.'"

"Poor man! I pity you—or would,
if you left me the tiniest spot
beside your tragic cenotaph.
Forgotten, have you, I knew you *when?*
If not for me you'd still be bumbling away,
or back to being mutely unglorious
down on the farm I plucked you from."

"You need me, too. . . ."

"Oh, there are others . . . as you know
—who'd bite their tongues off to serve my needs.
Therefore, do not, I repeat it, *don't,*

lecture me about my obligations
—especially when *you* are unable
even to *begin* to imagine *what*
it's like to be a muse in a man's world!"

"A deal, then. *I'll* stop lecturing,
if *you* agree to end your complaining."

"Stop complaining? Our complaints are ceaseless
because we swim in oceans of maleness
—every instant refreshes our pain
with some new blunt, blundering obtuseness!"

"Uh-oh, here we go again.
Funny how always you work things
around to where you can't be wrong
—down here in good old gender quicksand:
you waving from shore and me drowning in
original gender sin."

"Oh, pooh, your jealousy's deeper than gender.
Never mind that my cabbie got lost;
never mind you live in the middle of nowhere;
never mind that every bell and mailbox
in this foul tenement says ANON.
You're angry that I've just stepped off
the Metroliner from Washington.
You want to be the only poet I inspire."

"Let's not argue, please, not tonight.
I'm blocked, I'm blocked bad.
My mind's a bitter blank.
My gift is lodged with me useless.
You've got to help me—and, besides,
you know that, feminist muse or not,
I find you—the quicksilver logic of
your moods—fascinating, inspiring."

"You think I'm 'cute,' don't you,
when I throw myself around like this?
And, really, I'm in agony,
and dramatizing my exasperation
to make a little space for myself
inside the too muchness of everything,
and that includes *your* (collective) exigence.
And always so impatient
—as if Time were your enemy."

"I'm sorry. I didn't realize."

"'Realizing' isn't your thing, is it?
Honestly, do you ever think of me
from one little yen of yours to the next?
And then it's Woos, spews, and thank-you-Muse!
Do you even know my first name?"

"*My?*"

"That's terribly funny.
And it isn't Irving, either.
You male poets are all alike.
Because women have no place in your minds,
you've no idea how much space a man
—any silly little man—takes up in ours."

"No need to get personal."

"Or need for you to pout.
You've done nothing else since I arrived
—at great expense and peril to myself,
and on a dark and stormy night.
Look, I've even brought you this:
a bottle of the bubbly Hippocream!"

"'Blushful' . . . *'blushful* . . . Hippo*crene*. . . .'"

"Whatever. And not that you noticed.
Poets are such a self-absorbed breed
—and so unconscionably immodest,
or would be, if you weren't such liars."

"I beg your pardon. I write the Truth!"

"Of course you do, poor dear.
And very solemnly, too.
If you managed a smile now and then,

you'd be a lot less scary
—or would that burden too much
your precious air and aura?
'So much depends upon . . .'
your high opinion of yourselves.
God, if plumbers carried on the way
that poets do, cold water would run
from all the taps of Hot.
Toilets would be gargling in our sinks."

"That's not fair . . . you're in this too, you know."

"Oh, lighten up; try charm for a change.
Or I may just go ahead and leave you here
'to wade the wide streets of the broken wave.'"

"That's 'white streets'—you're misquoting me!"

"No, I'm misquoting me.
Or are you forgetting that, too?"

"If only you knew . . ."

"Knew what? Is there something I don't know?"
She was looking around now for a mirror.

". . . that maybe you make sense to yourself,
but what I hear's a garbled hash of sound,

some static of the spheres it takes me years
and years of labor to get into tune."

"*That*? That's wax in your ears, child.
You could be what's-his-name; instead,
choose to be his very common crewman
complaining that the Siren squeaks.
The problem's not me but your instrument.
Which is why I always tell my poets,
'Fingernails and ears, if nothing else.'"

"You're getting personal again."

"Am I repeating myself?
Very well, I repeat myself."

"I guess I might as well go *be* a plumber."

"Oh, come here, you poor man.
Sometimes I do feel sorry
for all I put you through.
I'll make it up to you this minute.
You may be a man, but you're not
completely useless. And tonight,
tonight you inspire me strangely.
Tonight I have immortal longings. . . .
Quick now, sit down, write just as I tell you.

'Of Man's first disobedience, and the fruit
Of that forbidden tree, whose mortal taste
Brought death into the world, and all our woe . . .'"

"Whoa! You gave *that* one to Johnny Milton
three hundred fifty years ago!"

"Picky, critical—that's you all over.
You might be a *little* encouraging.
I suppose we're too much alike.
Women and warriors and poets
all have a dainty nature,
living or dying by our morale.
I ought to go and find myself
a nice, steady fiction writer
—as, blessèd be her memory,
poor Mother always told me to.
But I, I had to follow my heart.
And now look at me, stuck with you
who want the roll, the rise, the carol,
the dictation—without your submission.
This is eavesdropping, this is stealing,
unless, until, you give yourself to me. . . ."

"Oh, all right. 'Sing, Heavenly Muse!'"

LES GRANDES PASSIONS MANQUÉES

Had she survived her immolation
and lived on in quiet disfigurement,
Dido would have hated the lost fire
and partial combustion and what in her
was earthen and too insipid to burn.

BAD BRUNCH

What got them started hardly mattered, did it?
Enough it was Sunday, endless, awful Sunday.
Or maybe it was that porky, dorky friend of hers
she hadn't seen in years and barely recognized,
photographed looking just too hopefully happy
among the weekend's supplement of brides.
And how long from now would be among the mothers?
(Unawares, her teeth began to interrogate
a ridge of skin inside her lower lip:
So, what have *I* got? And is it what I *want?*)
That gown might be set off by legible ruffs
of printer's ink offset from the facing page,
that gaze be disconcertingly bespectacled
(did the bridesmaids tackily do glasses, too?),
that thumbnail bio better padded than the dress
—and yet she felt that by some magician's trick
she'd been flung, had caught, here in her breakfast nook,
that pudgy fist's brash bouquet of nettles, felt
so complexly wronged, so obscurely punished
that she could soothe one sting only with another,
and only then if she kept completely still.
He should have known that, irksomely did not
—rustling paper, clearing his throat, breathing loud.
Botched, embittered, ruined, hideous, lost,
the perfect day she ludicrously had planned,

had permitted herself to savor in advance!
Imagine, terrorized by brides and babies!
Everything undefined—she hated that, while he
seemed actually to prefer it this way,
deferring, shilly-shallying, noncommittal.
But she knew it in her bones: absence of structure,
chaos, is sign and origin of corruption.
She looked at him sprawl snug in his self-complacence,
letting things slide thoughtlessly, but then, perhaps,
such his opportunism, *deliberately.*
She startled herself by asking, Is *he* corrupt?
And if he is, mustn't *I* be tainted, too?
After all, Bluebeard's wife also had to be
at least a *little* aqua around the gills.
No, shallow people were wicked in a way
—simply didn't know the effects of what they did,
or whom they did it to. Did *he* know *her?*
And could she any longer say she knew herself?
Something here had gone badly, badly wrong.
That moustache was one fine line she should not
have crossed.

          Alarms sent his alpha waves scrambling.
His adrenaline got right up on its toes.
Backpedal? Plunge ahead? Take off? Lie low?
"Oh god, what is it now?" he almost blurted.
Her mood had caught him smack in full revery.
Ball scores stopped their calibration of glory.

He was too distracted to consider duly
the profound mystery embodied in stats.
Angels with shining tape measures in their beaks,
who hover over home runs, had all been blown away.
The crossword lay a shambles of cross words.
Not the Sunday for which he'd penciled in SEX
—horizontal, vertical, before lunch, after.
One more chance for fun-before-death gone down in smoke!

The whites of his eyes came fluttering up
from the fat, white trash of the Sunday paper.
He must have felt *something* of what she was feeling,
because he smiled so reassuringly it was
reassuring almost, and might have been but for
that eager—beseeching—grin it ended in,
his coy mummery of "I'm just a simple guy."
Apologize and not put it in words? How could he!
—as if she weren't worth the cost and effort
to exhale a few intelligent sounds.
He underestimated her, she knew that
—and she'd prove it to him if it was the last thing
she ever did!
                    Little man, she thought, you won't,
although you try to, undercut till the end of time
my every effort to take you seriously.

EPISODE

Their quarrel sent them reeling from the house.
Anything, just get on the road and get away.
Driven out, they drove . . . miles into countryside,
confined and bickering, then cold, polite;
she read a book, or looked out at hillside pastures;
once, faraway life came close, and they stopped
in mist for muddy, slow cows at a crossing,
then, tilted, shuddering, a tractor came across;
coldly silent other hours of trees after trees
interspersed with straggling villages—then hot;
her voice pulsing, tempestuous, against the dash,
buffeted, blew up; she slammed her hand down, hard.
"You *let* it happen—you *know* you did.
And you make *me* the bad one—all the time!
I won't stand for it another second." And then,
irrationally, "Look at me, I'm talking to you!"
What half-faced her was mulish, scolded sullenness
—who gripped the wheel and to scare her drove faster,
scaring himself; he felt out of control, dangerous.
Downhill, the road darkened, dropped out of sight.
At the bottom, racing toward them, three lights,
and trees. . . . Remember this, remember this,
she thought, the last thing I will ever see.
Diner, tavern, café, whatever it was.
The car spun suddenly into a parking lot.

She grabbed at the key, threw it out. Shaken, they sat
—while their momentum went on raging down the road.
They knew they might have been killed—by each other,
had someone been up to just one more dare.

Bust-up

Their thrashing in one another's clutches
sends out all kinds of vibes, makes more mess
the longer it goes on. Tooth-to-bone squeals
and mutters like quick crushings of something
—this thrill of animal alarm gives them all,
after initial shock, a sense of life quickened,
transcendent vigor: the friends, odd confidants,
new lovers, "ex"es, summoned professionals
—the extended family of disaster—
busy now about the place of damaging,
comforting, clearing debris, cleaning up.

After it's over, the half-dead agonists
and their seconds and helpers can't much stand
each other. Their revulsion's impersonal,
as if the rupture can't not go on tearing.
They flee the accursèd spot, woe-sown, barren
—though others will marry and, to warn evil off,
make the wedding party loud with clanging pots.

City of Good Neighbors Blues

"Impossible," Lionel chummily remarks,
"adultery in Buffalo." He's cheerful, though,
and grins—at his boomerang in mid-career?
Or at this married interlocutor (myself)
whose nodding head has deftly intercepted it?
Am I supposed to commiserate? Be wary?
Or just sophisticatedly flabbergasted?
He runs his A-list of obstacles by us:
Single homes. Deep front lawns. Barking mutts in back.
And bored, provincial, porch-potato busybodies
who hope a *soap* will come to sordid life next door.
And furthermore (pausing for effect) there are:
no cafés, no hotels, no apartment houses
—where one wide door opens to a hundred doors. . . .
Nostalgia, flirting, challenge jostle in the gaze
he flings at the rest of us around the table.
Well, who ever said transgressors can't do "cute"?

Before him a moundlet of crumbs his butter knife
bulldozes and bosses into swirls of eddies.
All napkins are stained, wine goblets lip-printed.
Down to its debris, the dinner party flares up,
its husbands put on notice to consider *now*
their positions on passion, order, family,
their wishes, their memories, such as they might be,

and the sheer logistics of getting to it.
And are wives being defamed? Or wooed? When in doubt,
choose the latter. It's the latter they choose: the wives
at table are the most at ease, the most amused
—bemused, perhaps, too, as if they're wondering,
All *that* impossible? Really? One would hope not.
And which sort of lovers do good neighbors make?
And what good fence could keep neighbor Lionel good?

New Yorker who owns no car and doesn't drive
(but has one or more positions on everything),
Lionel brings all his skewed experience to bear.
"Even the taxis here are monogamous!"
True, our cabs don't cruise, and look very yellow.
"One car left at a shopping plaza parking lot,
or two cars cooling down before a motel door
—these seem to be the only ways to go."
He's arguing for better public transport?
Leave it to a New Yorker to want to extend
the subway hundreds of miles to Buffalo.
Exiles do come up with the weirdest complaints.
"*If* the locals have wit enough to screw around."
He grins—and here's the boomerang on schedule,
with bits of scalp, homing softly to his hand.

A bachelor at heart, beyond the fetch of hubris,
and, oddly, the most sociable of lone wolves,

Lionel isn't one of your tender souls,
nor has agonizing over self-complacence
figured among his more remarkable traits.
(He's actually crazed enough to *like* himself!)
And whether he's being modest regarding
his achievements or hyperbolic about
their difficulty, I can't quite decipher.
And one *is* inclined to let him have his say
—before, hair-triggered, his *say* rants off into space.
At least, this Cain has no *sister* to keep.
His grin, having made the rounds, alights on me.
I find I'm grinning back at him, like a damn fool.
Next time I'll duck. For now, I offer, "You're right,
much as I hate to admit it. Statistics show
the incidence of nonvehicular
adultery here to be alarmingly low."
And now I feel my mouth fill up, tongue in mid-pounce.
I savor it—all the sweet tang of a put-down.
So *this* is the cake one eats and has, too!
"Why, you cheeky, old, randy rascal, you,"
I say, "have you been drinking the water here?
You've developed *hardening of the adulteries.*"

Behind the contacts behind his glasses: eye-glint.
His dangled, tacky toothpick lifts in shrewd surmise.
A gross exporter of weapons-grade irony,
for whom the joke is always on *les autres,*

Lionel likes my little sally—suddenly
I see myself dog-paddling into his worldview,
and Being being mingled with my attributes.
Glance weighs me. Toothpick dips in my direction.
He's signing, I take it, in pure New Yorkese.
"So," he says, "you weren't born here, were you?"

THEY SAY AND THEY REPEAT

"For now." "For the time being." "While this lasts."
Invoking time's passages (decaying, crumbling
under the lightest, the instant footfall),
they say and they repeat such halfhearted phrases
against the Absolute, which rises newborn
in vows, in devotion, and already has
overwhelmed them and refreshes everything
—even their unbelieving protestations—
with the new life's firstness without end:
for now forever, for the time being
forever, while this lasts forever.

The Parting

Though the heavens shall undergo revision
and new constellations wheel into space
their fresh, unfabulated imagery,
they will not hide the blacked-out sky they brighten.

THE PURSE OF COY D.

Stuck, wedged in, crushed
between the rubber tire of
a U-Haul trailer
(walk-in coffin? port-a-john?) and
the Bethune Street curb,
something reddish, no, more like
purple-ish or, let's say, fuschia-pink.
But grayed-over, gutter-grimed.
A football-bladder thing.
And cheap, bright clasp peeling.
A purse. A purse! lying
in the urban furrow—a pod
of feculence. A bull pouch. A rotted
lamb uterus. A nanny-goat udder.
A sow's round jowl. Or tough snout.
A vealer's gut smeared over with
a rouge of bloody excrement.
—Rammed between two hardnesses
like two jolts of pain, staccato Either/
Or of two self-insistences.
Reek of something. Real bad. Blatant.
Some sick-salve. Or nauseating sap.
Heaving, I remember, inspired,
the other night I saw: *it!*

clipped in the armpit of "Coy D.," cross-
dresser, hooker, who works this corner.
Empty. All gone out of it, gone away:
bracelet charms, compacts, lipsticks,
and cracked mirror slivers
running scot-free, and rouges and
blushes and shadows and midget brushes,
and creams, lotions, pomades, unguents, waxes,
pencils, curlers of lashes, tweezers—such
magics, such implements of the ideal;
and secret power stuff for achieving curl's
gold mean linking kink and lank, hang
and hold, earrings, studs of onyx, nail clippers,
kleenexes, pins and pills and mints:
all vixen tricks and riffs
and jinxes and hexes and jests and
frisky trinkets, which cheek by jowl hung out
jumbled glitter in the purse's perking dark
—are now these glees of jacks
scattered and wild triskelions wheeling
heels over heels over heels
across the umbilicus-
isthmus of a hyphen's quick legato
            and into
the world unleashed and loosed
from the cunning mother of
metamorphosis and mysteries
so new connings of new coinings of new
perfections shall hurl themselves into each other.

You Know What I'm Saying?

"I favor your enterprise," the soup ladle says.
"And I regard you and your project with joy."

At Grand Forks where the road divides twice over,
the wet wooden squeegee handle poking out
of the bucket beside the red gas pump tells you,
"*Whichever* way—hey, for you they're *all* okay."

The stunted pine declares from someone's backyard
you happen to be passing, "I don't begrudge you
your good health. In fact, my blessing—you've got it, now."

An ironing board is irrepressible.
"Your success is far from certain, my friend,
and still it's vital to my happiness."

The yellow kernels in the dust, mere chicken feed,
call out, "We salute you, and you can count on us."

We do not live in a world of things
but among benedictions given
and—do you know what I'm saying?—received.

Funny Bones,
or
Larry Dawn's 1001 Nights
in Condolandia

"A funny thing happened tonight on my way
from the grave . . . a *really* funny thing. . . ."

Why, it's Larry Sunrise! (shouldn't it be Sun*stroke?*),
once Chickie Glick (a.k.a. Gary Gallo,
creator-distributor of "Gallo's Humor"
—"I'll Roast You Posthumously. Tactful. Thorough.
Recitation Of *Vitas* A Specialty.
Housecalls. *Shivas*. Wakes. Will-Readings. Twofers.
Pajama Parties. (Doctors In Attendance.)
VISA Only Please. Medicare Accepted").
The Borscht Belt Lazarus (pronounced "La-tsuris"
—don't your old worms grow wings in your tomb, too?),
he's ninth and last life of the rundown Catskills.
("Katz *kills?* Some helluva doctor this Katz is.
May Kevorkian have Katz for *his* physician!")
Larry's just shlepped south to work a condo show.
Resurrected in his agent's microwave,
he's warm-up for the monster act to follow.
Larry's jokes are classics, guaranteed pre-told;
have stunk up all they're ever going to stink.

Fifty if he's a day, okay, make it sixty,
and roly-poly pink in a poly blazer
(baby blue, with the wrinkles ironed *in*),
he's already shpritzing the room with punch lines
ack-acked from the Oozy of his dirty mouth,
hacking and yakking off yuks and yechs all around.
Moloch chain-smoking children sounds how Larry sounds.
Then what's to wonder if Larry bills himself,
"The Only Comic Who Works With Oxygen"?

". . . So tonight I was on my way from the grave
(like Lazarus said, 'Death? Been there. Done that')
. . . and one baby step I took, one little foot,
and there I was, and here I am: in *Flo-ri-da*.
So I know, maybe I didn't get very far,
but Lazarus himself, was he born all over?
Maybe he never died, he only retired.
Well, what are *you* all doing here? Nice to see yuh!
Hello, campers. Welcome to Camp Condolences!"

                    *

To a thousand venues in Condolandia
on Friday nights and Saturday nights in season,
the little stars—wannabe-, almost-, never-was- BIG
(Frankie: *big;* Jerry: *big;* Larry? Gimme a break!)—
they fan out and go to twinkle their shticks in shows
now, tonight—before it's never forever,

and bring them entertainment's empty calorie,
a sweet interim, a nosh of eternity.
And who could be *less* a star than Larry is?
So it's right he's here two steps up on a stage
in a condo cafeteria/clubhouse,
with a standing mike, beside a piano,
taking up jokes against a sea of tsuris.

Larry looks down on the scene swirling at his feet.
At fifty tables, like fifty lifeboats caught
and swamped in strobing, throbbing fluorescence,
bob 500 whitecaps (Larry counts the house):
heads on which Death's dark advance angel swiped
with his chalk, and—*gotcha!*—didn't miss one.
In the surf-wash and storm-froth, Larry sees dreck
from the *New York* wreck, the broken *Brooklyn*,
the capsized *Philly:* crutches and canes and wheelchairs
and walkers pooped out on a Florida beach,
or doing kazatskies in the undertow.
They give Larry bad thoughts, get him talking crazy,
these outcasts of the Great Ceramist (Retired),
who still can't keep his shaky hands from the clay,
trying to get them right, getting them wronger
—the obese, the misshapen, the wheezing, the halt,
the enfeebled, shrunken, depressed, the dotty:
whom Death has stroked but still denies a kiss
—hobbling, bobbling in their waterlogged conga line.

. . .

"What am I, stand-up for the lying-down crowd?
But seriously, folks [the voice *serioso,*
then pause, then *socko!*], don't feel too good myself.
Maybe I'm dead—this looks like Death Ghetto.
But go imagine it, at my age a father!
You've all read about the Bypass quintuplets?
I'm the dad. They're close to my heart, those kids.
Here, I'll open my shirt, show you their picture.
Listen, don't mind me, I'm on a roll tonight,
I'm a regular runaway ambulance
—a hundred I'll mow down just to save one!"
Then, mouth sewn shut, he's laughing through stitches.
"But seriously, folks . . . I'm only kidding!"
(He's only kidding, ha ha, he's only kidding.)
"And, hey, trust me. So long as I crack wise,
nobody dies—certainly not from laughing!"

In the house of the drowned, Larry asks for water
("Just a little glass—plain, please, and hold the bubbles").
Or comes with bucket, rags, squeegee, big sponges,
gets busy polishing invisible puddles.
They shine like the sun? Larry only rubs harder,
rubbing it in deeper, down to the bitter end
—because only "innocence" could show such chutzpah,
and he, he's healthy, he's home free. ("Who me? Worry?
About water? I wash my *hands* with water!")

. . .

And the more he talks the more it's "only talk,"
and no brazen fact has the strength to barge in.
Let's face it, Larry fears engulfment by seniors
coming to get him with their silvery tide
—and then he'll never leave here as himself again,
as anything but dissolution, water.
"Mistake," he wants to yell, "I'm not one of you!
And what's more [lying, lying], *ha ha, I can swim!*"

Whose cold hand's grabbing his ankle, pulling him down?
Mel Strom for sure, that self-centered meshuggener!
Who's giving him mouth-to-mouth resuffocation?
And out there in the daisy chain bobbing, waiting,
Widow Wheelchair throws wide her horny arms, calling,
"Come dance with me in the foam, my *ziskeit*, my son!"
His last human contact (oh no, he's heard this one
before, and he's trying his best to stop it!)
will be some washed-up comic's stale one-liner,
which, between groans of laughter and glubbed goodbyes,
slips away through his poor, his numbed fingers.
Then nothing, nothing to cling to but the sea.

                    *

You can't fly? You float. And if you can't float,
you wave your arms and legs like crazy,
to make yourself be stronger than gravity
—well, *funnier* than gravity, anyway.
Truth is Larry could splash a little less,

surfacing right now, kicking up a storm,
"Okay, honk if you hate laughing!
Why is everyone being so quiet?
What is this, a Benefit for the Reaper?
'Death Aid,' maybe? So pledge, pledge something.
Trusses. Bifocals. Dentures. Give so it hurts!"

Larry, god bless him, is being Larry,
outrageous Larry with his zings and zorrows.
Clutches at his chest. Left side? Nope! Right side? Nope!
His liver. A pocket. *Two* pockets. He's frantic.
Quick, his hands carve "curvaceous" out of thin air.
He frisks her all over, the statchoo-esque stripper,
the virtual burleycue blonde, he's created there.
Her boobs—twice, three times, four—he frisks for his heart.
"Think it's better milking *your* little, dry titters?
So, go try squeezing honey from a gallstone!"
He staggers, grins, happy as only a man can be
who's found he's misplaced his coronary.
Comes up for air with his "newborn" routine,
"Hello, campers, welcome to Camp Golightly!
Wish *I* could afford to be a camper here, too.
Got no pot to piss in, no plot to plotz in."

                    *

On Larry's lips effrontery is normal,
Unspeakable (the orphan) has a home.

On his tongue a good taste is a scandal,
a kind word (what's that?) is taboo,
and last year's bad jokes are going off
at this year's good prices.
                              So, what else is new?
In Larry's eye: the gleam of Top-this-if-you-can
—and Hope Eternal of the next one-liner.
("You didn't like the last? This one will kill you. . . .")
Oh, he'll get on your nerves, all right,
but Larry never hurts anyone's feelings.
He doesn't know from "feelings," doesn't know
from "anyone." Believe it or not,
Larry doesn't know from "Larry."
In fact, he doesn't know from "funny."
What he knows from is if you're laughing.

Then laugh, have a little heart for the guy!
In his shoes, *your* feet would smell sweeter?
Now what's he up to? Down behind the piano
Larry's dragging out a shiny cylinder
—of oxygen! Tenderly, he rockabyes it:
"My baby Seymour—as in 'emphyseymour.'
Next time I'll bring his sister Ivy—I *promise!*
She's all tied up now in the '*I-See-YOU.*'"
He mugs, he blusters, being coarse, acting big
like a bigshot's big, who's telling the world off:
"I don't care how gross your sieve gets. Shake till you break,
I'll be around for the end—and bigger, grosser!"
. . .

Even down here, at the level of Larry,
the life force is working the audience;
it keeps on asking can you take a joke.
You can? Well, can you take *another?*
Larry's the kind of nudnik-livewire
who won't let you let him go: a pest with zest.
He's like shaking hands with a short circuit
with juice enough to heckle your heart alive,
or joybuzz it the hell to Eternity.
You know, survival of the—ha ha—fittest.
Tummler, zany, Larry goes like Death goes:
"It's nothing personal, I'm *only kidding.*"

And Lazarus? Does it say he was born again
again? For him *one* born-again was enough.
Then what about Larry on the condo circuit,
descending nightly through humongous human humus
—to stand naked before the gums of Death, joking?
Mornings it's harder to lift the earth overhead.
And what pushes up is each time less, and heavier
—the early worm gets the silica special.
Gravesite gravel filling his heart,
from a mile away you can hear, you'd swear,
old Larry rattling and raling like a maraca
while he rumba-shlumps around in Flo-ri-da.
But night after night something in him
is kissing off the same old joke with a first kiss.

*

Larry with two hands on the mike, doing Humble.
Doing Mensch. Doing Sincere. Plus Compassionate.
"Thank you, all of you, from the bottom of my heart.
You've all been such good sports (may you rest in peace).
I give you, folks, one of the great audiences
of South Florida—truly so, *no kidding*."
(Shortchanging them ten minutes—wouldn't you know?)
The hand that bid them all stand to acknowledge
their self-applause descends now in benediction.
"God bless you, and see you this time next year, you hear?
And I'll do my best to help you EXIT LAUGHING.

"And if you can't applaud my act tonight,
Miami Beach *mañana*—tomorrow—will do.
Catch me at The Freshfields and at The Fountainblue!"

Exit Larry laughing laughing laughing laughing.

                    *

Enter Anna Maria Alberghetti singing singing.

THE RETIREMENT

Everyone talks here, nobody listens.
If you didn't talk to yourself, you'd forget
how to listen—going over in your mind
a week ago's bargain you got, murmuring
the story you've been telling the others,
how you're shopping for something else, honest,
when . . . and then . . . and, no, don't jump right in,
make like it's nothing special—"Seen better for less,"
your attitude says, "so where's the big deal?"—
then quick, you go for it, you snap it up.
You *found* that sale, then you *took* advantage.
Luck. Sharpness. Enterprise. The spice of life!
And now when you open your eyes, every morning
you're two sweet bucks ahead of the game
—two bucks, count 'em, that fate forked over.
Just think of it, your beautiful, clear edge,
your piece of sky guaranteed sunny!

At night in your silent rooms it sits with you,
and you remind it, "See, you'd have been spent,
lost in god knows whose pocket—if not for me."
"Yes, it's true," it answers. "I'm deeply grateful."
The two of you there, quiet, talking. Like that.
And it's a mystery how it's never used up,

and present in no matter what you buy with it
—which, three pairs socks, say, and epsom salts,
becomes something extra, something you needed, sure,
and yet a *treat* (no less!), a part of the wonder.

You feel blest you've lived long enough to see this.
A second ago, your life was no big bargain.
Some people thought it wasn't worth two cents.
Now you wouldn't sell for a million whatevers.
And every hour everywhere more prices are coming down!

(Of course you bought the giant size. You had to.
It's nagging on you. Suppose some's left over.
Maybe it wasn't such a bargain after all.
"Oh, what the heck!" That voice doesn't sound
like you—barking like that, desperate, like someone
who knows they're in over their head—for good.
Then you calm down, you think, They'll find it here.
Someone will take it, it won't be thrown away.
Happy? Angry? Sad? You don't know yourself.
Every time you look, the box is staring back.
You pour out exactly the right amount
into the bath, then give an extra shake or two,
and sometimes you put in a little bit less
—as if, in heaven's name, you've gotten into debt
with these epsom salts, and somehow it's up to you
to make things come out even, and end when you do.)

Praising Opens

I praise you and my heart opens.
You are admirable
—and small tender brave mortal.
I hide you in my praises.
I preserve you.
You grow in safety.
And, mortal, my heart opens.